IMAGES
of England

WARWICK

Fanny Cardall as a young woman. She was born in 1836 and married George Cashmore of Warwick. They had a large family but sadly Fanny died giving birth to their sixth child, Samuel, when she was only thirty-three.`

IMAGES
of England

WARWICK

Compiled by
Jacqueline Cameron

TEMPUS

First published 2000
Copyright © Jacqueline Cameron, 2000

Tempus Publishing Limited
The Mill, Brimscombe Port,
Stroud, Gloucestershire, GL5 2QG

ISBN 0 7524 1877 7

Typesetting and origination by
Tempus Publishing Limited
Printed in Great Britain by
Midway Clark Printing, Wiltshire

*This book is dedicated to Jack and Molly Cox, the author's parents,
who made it all possible.*

The Lover's Seat near Guy's Cliff Mill, *c.* 1910.

Contents

Acknowledgements

Graham Wilton for his help with the photography, Margaret Gurney, Betty Walters, June Haynes, Jackie and Georgina Turpin, Mrs Eileen Bewley, Roy Davies JP, Councillor Bob Attwood, Malcolm Loveridge, Ron Cashmore and wife, Mrs Pam Bull and Molly Cox. Photographs supplied by Warwickshire County Council, Department of Libraries and Heritage Warwickshire Collection, Mrs M. Simpson, Clifford Dillow and David Harwood, The Warwick Records Office, Andrew Wild Snr, Andrew Wild Jnr, and John Whitmore.

The marriage of Muriel James to George Pankhurst, 21 September 1940. Muriel arrives for the wedding accompanied by her brother, Alfred.

Introduction

I felt very honoured when I was given the opportunity to write this book on Warwick and privileged to be able to recall the memories of the place where I was born and the people who not only made my childhood a happy one, but moulded Warwick into the town as we know today.

Of the history of Warwick, much has been written about Warwick Castle over the years, which is one of the finest medieval castles in England and dates back to 1068, two years after the Norman conquest. First structured in timber at the time of William I, the motte and bailey castle was to be used as a strong point on his march north to quell an insurrection and was destined to play an important part throughout Warwick's history.

During its lifetime the castle has been altered from a timber building into stone and had two magnificent towers, Caesar's and Guy's, built in the fourteenth century, thanks to the generosity of the de Beauchamps. The massive gatehouses and barbican between them are also due to the same benefactor and to this day thrill each visitor to pass through what used to be the Vineyard Garden.

Over the years the castle was to change hands many times, owned by such well known figures as Sir Fulke Greville, descendant of William Greville of Chipping Campden and the Earls of Warwick. It is currently in the possession of Madam Tussauds who acquired the castle and many of its contents in 1978. It wasn't until 1816 that the castle was first opened to the public on a regular basis, chiefly for the benefits of nobility and gentry, but it's interesting to note that the castle is now open every day except Christmas Day for everyone to enjoy.

The great fire was also to have a lasting effect on the town's history with 250 houses destroyed or damaged by the fire in September 1694. The seriousness of the blaze was attributed to so much thatch and timber about the town.

As you enter Warwick you cannot help but notice the East and Westgates which mark part of the medieval defences of the town. Both gates have a short length of genuine town wall attached to them, and above the Eastgate can be found St Peter's chapel, which started its life as a small parish church near the centre of the town, but was rebuilt over the Eastgate in the fifteenth century. Above the Westgate is the chapel of St James. Both the gates are in excellent condition and even to this day one walks through the gates on cobbles which are probably as old as the gates themselves. As a child I used to love to run through them and listen to the echo of my shoes in the archways!

The town is dominated by the castle but also by St Mary's church and Beauchamp chapel. The tower was rebuilt from sandstone quarried from the churchyard after the 1694 fire, to the design of Sir William Wilson and stands 155 feet high. Inside the church, in the chapel, is the tomb of Robert Dudley, Earl of Leicester, surrounded by Paris ironwork. In the centre of the chapel is a monument to Richard Beauchamp, the founder.

No introduction to the town would be complete without mentioning the Lord Leycester Hospital, and the Malthouse, which is the Elizabethan building leading to the gate of the Lord Leycester Hospital itself. The courtyard can be found at the centre of the medieval guild properties in which the Master and Brethren were installed. The Banqueting Hall is famous as the place where James I was entertained by Sir Fulke Greville of Warwick Castle. The Masters House is decorated with amusing little figures: Warwick bears, ragged staves at varying angles, Dudley's double-tailed lion, an arrow of Sidney Kinsfolk and the famous porcupine are just a few of the interesting items to be found in the hospital.

Warwick has many historic buildings, boasting among them the Market Hall and Museum which was erected for the borough by a local builder William Hurlbutt in 1670, and the Abbotsford which stands at the north end of the Market Place and was built in 1714 to replace the Bull Inn. Okens House in Castle Street is an attractive medieval timber-framed building, which narrowly escaped the great fire and was home to Thomas Oken, a famous benefactor of Warwick. St John's House, which stands on the site of a medieval hospital and was built by Anthony Stoughton in 1626, is now a branch of the County Museum, and houses the Royal Warwickshire Regimental Museum.

Alas, as much as I love my fellow Warwickeans, our forefathers were not above reproach – Warwick prison bears witness to this. The original building in Northgate Street, found to be a serious danger to the health of prisoners and warders alike, was abandoned in 1860 for a newly built prison at the Cape. This prison was purpose built with 2 yards, 4 dayrooms and 309 cells for criminals, and 4 yards, 3 dayrooms and 43 sleeping rooms for debtors!

Warwick Priory, which no longer stands in the Priory Park, was much altered and greatly extended during its lifetime in England. Older than St John's in origin, it incorporated the stones of the actual Priory of St Sepulchre. Unfortunately, a sale in 1925 of the Elizabethan and Jacobean shell of the Priory resulted in it being purchased by Mr and Mrs Alexander Willbourne Weddell, the former American Ambassador to Spain, and the Priory's ultimate destination was Richmond, Virginia. The Weddell's used the material for the erection of their home, Virginia House, at Windsor Farms. The property is now in the hands of the Virginia Historical Society, after the tragic death of the Weddells in a railway accident in 1948.

Also to be mentioned is Guy's Cliffe House, which stands on a steep slope overlooking the River Avon. Very much a ruin, this once magnificent house was reported to have been the place where the legendary Guy of Warwick retired as a hermit. The chapel here goes back in part to the twelfth century and thanks to Richard Beauchamp, Earl of Warwick, the house was largely rebuilt in 1422.

Warwick is famous for its annual Mop, which is the only traditional fair to survive to the present time. The first fair in Warwick was held in 1261, when John du Plesses was given permission to hold a fair for eight days around the feast of St Peter and vanicula. Originally a hiring fair, it still brings back many lovely memories of childhood to Warwick inhabitants. The days when the Mop visited the town each year, and stories of the time the big wheel got stuck and town folk spent many hours as prisoners of the wheel throughout the night, still enthrall me to this day. So does the reintroduction of the hog roast, and the queue I stood in while mother purchased a roll so that we could taste 'what it used to be like'!

In conclusion, I have to say that Warwick will always have a special place in my heart, because of the host of shopkeepers and characters around the town that I remember: the smell of the coffee from Thackers and Christmas, the lovely pork from Chadbands the pork butchers in Swan Street, Ben Cowley the butcher who always gave me half a pound of cooked meat but charged me for a quarter, Chris Jones, who for many years sold fruit in the Market Square, Pratts the chemist, Hatton's which I remember for the money that used to disappear in little boxes across the ceiling from the counter to the cashier and return with your change in! The Liquorice Factory in Theatre Street, where we used, as children, to always manage to scrounge a little square of liquorice on our way home from school. Mr Vittle the undertaker, Mr Cohen Senior the dentist and Mr Mulligan the doctor were part of my childhood memories of the town, as were Messrs Hunt and Dillow the coalmen, and Mabel Buswell and her father, who kept us all supplied with fresh vegetables, delivered to the house, from their horse and cart. As well as old views of the streets and buildings of Warwick, you will also meet, in these pages, a host of Warwick people. All have one thing in common, they helped make Warwick the town it is today.

One
The Shire Town

Eastgate and Landor House, 1900s. A disastrous fire in 1694 destroyed most of the centre of Warwick but buildings around the periphery of the town survived the conflagration and many of these remain to this day. Landor House was built just before the fire and, like other buildings in this view, survived. Landor House is now part of a girls' school. The house bears the name of one of Warwick's distinguished sons, Walter Savage Landor, poet and essayist.

Eastgate seen from inside the walls, *c.* 1905.

The Eastgate is one of three main gate entries into the town. The others are on the north and west sides. The Eastgate was probably constructed in the fifteenth century and has the chapel of St Peter built over it. The Eastgate has a wide arch over the original roadway and a smaller one for pedestrians. On the left is the Porridge Pot which was a popular, high class cafe when this postcard view was taken, probably in the 1930s. The Eastgate now forms part of Kings High School for girls and the Porridge Pot has become pizza parlour.

St John's House, originally the hospital of St John the Baptist founded here in the reign of Henry II. The building, consisting of a gatehouse, chapel and two houses, was intended for the use of the homeless, poor and travelling strangers. The buildings changed their use several times and in 1780 was sold to the Earl of Warwick in whose family it remained until 1960. It was a school between 1791 and 1881 and became, in 1924, a Military Record and Pay Office. It is currently a branch of the county museum and museum of the Warwickshire Regiment.

This photograph of the Holloway brings back happy memories of my childhood. We passed along here on our way to school, a road also known locally as 'the Rock' because it was constructed from the underlying rock surface.

Warwick gasworks. This elegant building with two cupolas can still be seen today.

This scene in the Market Place is from around 1910. The International Stores is alas no more. Notice the hardware shop's display of wares on the road and pavement.

A picturesque view of the lovely Guy's Clff Mill from a postcard sent in 1904 by someone who calls herself 'Mollie B'. At this time there was only space for writing a short message on the front of postcards as the whole of the back was used for the address.

A back view of Guy's Cliff Mill from the river in around 1910.

As children we used to love to run across this wooden bridge that leads to the old mill, then pause to look for fish in the water below.

This delightful photograph of Guy's Cliff Mill in the 1900s shows the building still in use as a working mill with a horse and wagon loaded up with sacks and 'ready for the off'.

This old view looks into Castle Lane which skirts around the edges of the castle grounds.

Mill Street also adjoins the castle grounds and is still perhaps one of the prettiest streets in Warwick. This scene is taken from a postcard photograph of around 1906.

A view through the arch along the river Avon to Warwick castle. On the right are boats that belonged to thje Warwick boathouse. These boats were available for hire and on sunny days and Sundays were in high demand.

An old view of Warwick castle seen from the bridge which crosses the Avon from Banbury. This is the first impression that visitors approaching from this side get of the castle.

16

The splendid Caesar's Tower, Warwick castle, built during the fourteenth century and at the time of the de Beauchamp earls. None of the present castle buildings date from before the thirteenth century but there is clear evidence of the earlier motte and bailey construction that preceded the one we see today. Warwick castle is one of the finest surviving fortress houses to be seen anywhere.

This south front view of the castle was depicted in one of several famous painting by the Italian eighteenth-century artist Antonio Canale.

The castle courtyard in the 1920s. The castle is a popular attraction for visitors from all over the world and is still the home of the Earls of Warwick.

Another fine view from the castle courtyard taken in the 1920s.

WARWICK CASTLE, THE ITALIAN GARDEN

The Italian Garden at the castle depicted in a watercolour painting used as a postcard of the 1930s. Notice the peacock on the lawn: these beautiful birds have played a part in Warwick's history as the castle has been home to them for many years and it is not uncommon today to find them taking a stroll down the High Street. The castle grounds were landscaped by Capability Brown who began work here in 1753.

An old view from inside the castle gateway.

PRISONER'S PATH. WARWICK CASTLE.   105.

The infamous Prisoner's Path at the castle.
This photograph was produced as a postcard
for exclusive sale at The Porridge Pot cafe in
Eastgate (see p. 18).

An aerial view of Warwick casle showing its beautiful setting by the river. The bridge in the foreground of this view, when built, provided the first alternative river crossing near the castle since an earlier one was built in the thirteenth century.

Bridge End is an area across the river from the castle which looms romantically in the background of this photograph taken in the 1950s. Many of these old houses look much the same today.

A glimpse of old Warwick from a postcard view of around 1912. Part of the castle walls can be seen on the left.

A view of the Holloway from outside the Rose and Crown. The white building in the centre was the police station in Barrack Street and is now the public library.

Market Street and the water tower, c. 1910. The tower was demolished in 1923. Fletchers Stores is on the left and on the right, set back slightly behind a shop window blind, is the Corn Market.

The Corn Market, or Corn Exchange as it was called at the time of this photograph, opened in 1856. Early motion pictures were shown here in 1908. The shop on the right is Whittaker's fish and chip shop. The Corn Market became a branch of Woolworths for a time but the site is now a branch of W.H.Smiths.

The avenue of trees leading to Guy's Cliff House which stands on a steep slope overlooking the Avon. It is to this estate that the legendary Guy of Warwick is supposed to have retired. This view is taken from a coloured postcard photograph from around 1906. The reverse of this card carries a Christmas Greeting.

A view of the magnificient Guy's Cliff House, built in 1751, which stands one and a half miles northeast of the town. The house is now a ruin. Its demise was apparently assisted by a fire that started after a film crew were filming there.

This lovely black and white timbered building at the corner of Swan Street and New Street probably dates back to 1636. At the time of this photograph, in around 1960, it was a drapers known as the Beehive. As a child I can remember going there to buy wool for my mother. It now houses a travel agent.

Visitors, as they approach the Eastgate en route to the castle, cannot fail to notice this unusual red pillar box. A plaque nearby reads, 'This pillar box cast in 1856 in the shape of a Doric column at the Eagle Foundry of Messrs Smith and Hawkes, Broad Street, Birmingham, is one of a pair installed at the East and Westgates of Warwick.' The box featured on a set of stamps to commemorate post boxes of note.

A wintry scene on the river Avon as it winds its way past St Nicholas Park. The banks are still a well used walk today.

An old view of Warwick School built in the 1870s by J. Cundall.

Westgate from a coloured postcard photograph of around 1910.

The famous Lord Leycester's Hospital at Westgate from a postcard view of around 1900. No account of Warwick would be complete without inclusion of this wonderful architectural survivor from Elizabethan times. Originally the Guild House of St George in the fourteenth century it was largely rebuilt in 1571, after the Dissolution, by Robert Dudley, Earl of Leicester as almshouses for the old and disabled 'bretheren'; soldiers who had served with the earls. It survived the great Warwick fire of 1694 and can still be seen in all its glory today.

The courtyard of Lord Leycester's Hospital in the 1930s. Today the Hospital still houses twelve bretheren and a master, in quarters that have been modernized but are in keeping with the rest of the building. The kitchen, the banqueting hall and the chapel are all beautifully preserved.

Warwick's Westgate with the fifteenth-century chapel of St James built over it. Lord Leycester's Hospital is tucked in just beside it on the right.

St Mary's church in Northgate Street from a postcard view of around 1910. A church on this site is first recorded in 1086 but the original Norman and fourteenth-century building was largely destroyed in the great fire of 1694 and only the crypt, the chancel and south transept survive from it to give an idea of its original grand style. The rebuilding in the late seventeenth century, however, produced a beautiful new church and is a splendid example of Perpendicular style. The Beauchamp chapel is famous and the magnificent marble tomb of Richard Beauchamp, Earl of Warwick, who was a great figure in the Middle Ages, can still be seen in the centre of the church. The tower is open to visitors and gives a panaromic view over Warwickshire. As a child I can remember when the chimes of the clock were reintroduced and hearing 'Warwickshire Lads and Lasses' for the first time.

The stream in Warwick Park under a layer of snow and ice. In the centre of the picture one can just see the cafe and on the right are the childrens' swings. This stream, being fairly shallow and full of minnows, provided much summer entertainment for children.

No account of Warwick would be complete without mention of Piers Gaveston, whose monument can be found at Leek Wootton on Blacklow Hill, just a mile from Warwick. Piers Gaveston was made Earl of Cornwall in 1307, but unfortunately he was to make more enemies than was good for him. He was captured by the Earl of Warwick, tried at Warwick castle and sentenced to death. The monument marks the place where he was beheaded on 19 June 1312.

Two
Working Life

Mr Federick Skelsey at the railway where he worked, *c.* 1900.

Local coalman, Vic Dillow (right) delivering coal in Cape Road in the late 1940s.

George Cashmore was once a familiar sight in the early 1900s delivering bread for the family business with this handcart.

Supercar manufactured fairground rides in Warwick. This 1953 photograph shows Pat Walters, Jack Groves, John French and Jack Walters on one of the rides that were their trademark.

Pat Walters driving a lorry for Supercar in the 1960s.

A group of young Warwick miners pose by the pit in 1916.

The International Stores in 1924. The man on the extreme right is Thomas Reeves and the lady is Gertrude Perry.

A group of Coventry and District Co-op store managers in the Co-op meeting rooms, Coten End in 1934.

A visit by branch managers of the Coventry and Hull Co-operative Societies to the CWS factory at Lowestoft. In the group is James Marshall Davies who managed Warwick Co-op stores.

The Warwick Laundry in St Nicholas Park, seen here, probably, in the late 1920s. Imagine the hot smell of ironing that there must have been in this room!

'Granny' Taylor in a studio portrait from the 1890s. As a young woman she worked at the laundry in St Nicholas Park.

These ladies, probably dressed up here for an outing, sometime around 1914, worked at the Warwick cigar factory on Castle Hill. The girls would look for news from the front during the First World War which was posted on a board in Castle Hill.

Left: Johnny Haynes, engine driver, undertakes a little repair work in 1939. It was a common sight in the days of steam to see the driver and fireman working side by side together in the engine cab as it rushed by. I can remember as a young child lying in bed on foggy nights and listening to the engines whistle as they ran down Hatton Hill into Warwick.
Right: Recasting the bells of St Nicholas' church in the 1930s.

No collection of photographs of Warwick would be complete without one of Jim Attwood who was the local Midland Red bus driver for many years. This was at the time when we would, as children, pay a penny ha'penny return to Leamington Spa. Jim's son Bob is now Cllr Attwod.

These are the Maclyn brothers who ran the Maclyn Café in Smith Street in the 1950s. Sylvia Haynes and Mrs Lines, who worked there, are also in the picture.

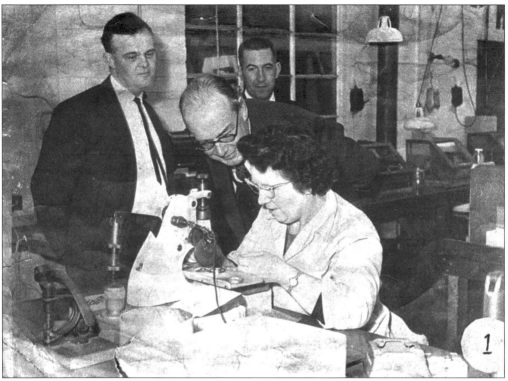

Mrs Rhoda Garrison demonstrates to visitors the making of castings for rings at Niagra Falls Castings, c. 1975.

Landlady Marge Harris (formerly Wood) with Rita March behind the bar at the Wheatsheaf in 1950.

This gathering at the Railway Depot in Leamington in the 1950s is a bit of a mystery. The engine bears a special number and is called The William Shakespeare making it look like a special excursion train but who are the men? The engine driver was John Haines of Warwick. Some of the others are clearly railwaymen because they are in uniform – but the others?

A Christmas office party at Turrifs, the construction firm, in Warwick.

George Cashmore with his son Samuel. George farmed at Budbrooke and was the local butcher. His shop was at the Old Wharf.

The Warwick Womens' Army Corps during the First World War. Fourth from the left, back row is Maud Staines.

The Warwick Home Guard in the 1940s.

Three
Sport and Leisure

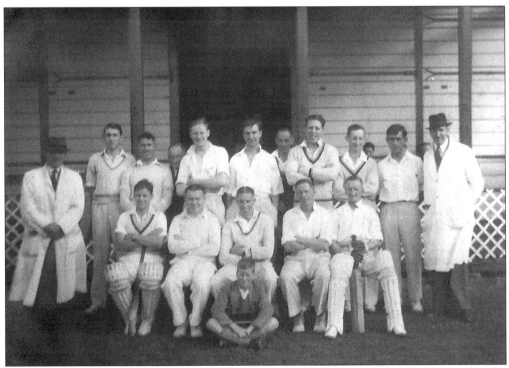

A pre-war photograph of a Warwick Cricket Club team at the Eagle sports ground in Hampton Road.

Warwick's famous sons. Dick Turpin was to make British boxing history by becoming the first non-white man to win a British title and Lonsdale Belt when he defeated Vince Hawkins and won the British Empire Middleweight Championship.

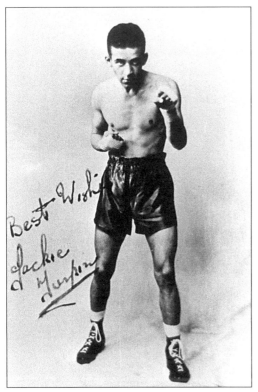

Dick's brother Jackie (above left) continued the family tradition by becoming the Midlands Area Featherweight Champion and number one contender for the British Featherweight title. Since retiring Jackie has coached at several clubs and still coaches at Warwick Racing Amateur Boxing Club. Not to be outdone by his famous brothers, Randolph Turpin (above right and right) became the first British World Middleweight Champion in sixty years when he beat Sugar Ray Robinson, the undisputed World Champion, on 12 September 1951. Sadly, Randolph died following a shooting incident in 1966.

A Warwick Football Club match in the 1950s with the referee George Pankhurst tossing the coin.

Hampton on the Hill football team, 1921/2. Only the players in the front row are known and they are, left to right: E. Tracy, T. Collett, G. Bourton, B. Vincent, T. Field.

Boatman Samuel Bissell stands on his boat by the tethered ferry across the Avon, 1900s.

A scene from an early Warwick pageant, probably around 1910. An inscription on this postcard tells us that this enactment depicts, 'Myfanwy appealing to Caradoc for the release of her child'.

Teachers in fancy dress at Milverton school, Greathead Road, *c.* 1900.

This photograph of James Marshall Davies was taken by his brother in 1921.

This Davis family group was recorded in their garden at Paradise Street in the 1920s. From left to right they are: Phil, Emily, Ivy and Stan.

A wet day in the High Street in the 1920s. In the photograph, from left to right, are: Phillip and Emily Davies, Miss and Mrs Gibbs.

Samuel Cashmore with his car on a visit to Hidcote Boyce in the early 1920s.

John Cashmore and Cyril Carvell are pictured with the family car in Warwick in the early 1930s.

Rhoda Garrison enjoying a ride on her motorbike. The photograph was, of course, taken in a photographer's studio with a painted backcloth. Many photographers kept a range of 'props' to add interest to studio photographs, especially at seaside resorts. This one was taken when Rhoda was on holiday in Blackpool in the 1930s.

Three sisters wearing the finest of 1920's headgear! They are Ivy, Rhoda and Phyllis Skelsey.

A dance troupe called the Nig Nogs performing here in Warwick in 1932. The troupe was organised by Marjorie Simmonds. Evelyn Reeves, who was twelve at the time, is second from the right.

The celebrations for George V's Silver Jubilee took place on 11 May 1935 in the grounds of Warwick castle. The brilliant floodlighting and fireworks display attracted huge crowds to the town whose streets were adorned with masses of flags and bunting. Around twenty thousand gathered in St Nicholas Park to watch the firework display and the bonfire that is said to have had flames reaching sixty feet into the air. Apparently the display was slow to get started which resulted in some shouting and clapping but once it began it was spectacular and incorporated, in fire, the words, '1910-1935 Long to Reign Over Us'.

This delightful photograph of the Cashmore family and friends was taken during a day's outing to the country. From left to right they are: Ethel Eden with the dog, Cyril Carvell, Florence, Gertrude and John Cashmore, Jim Eden, Walter Haines, Sarah, Samuel and Margaret Cashmore, Sheila Carvell, Florence and Ron Cashmore.

Maud Staines is pictured here on the Hampton Road with her bicycle in the 1930s.

Children at the VE Day celebrations in Warwick in 1945. From left to right: Derek Howells, Margaret Garrison and Brian Howells.

Tommy and Janet Bewley enjoy a ride on Blossom, the family's docile cart-horse in the 1940s.

King George VI and Queen Elizabeth on their visit to Warwick castle on 5 April 1951.

Warwick Mop has been an important date in the Warwick social calendar for a very long time. Pictured here at the Mop Fair in 1951 are, from left to right: William, Gwen, Brenda and Malcolm Loveridge.

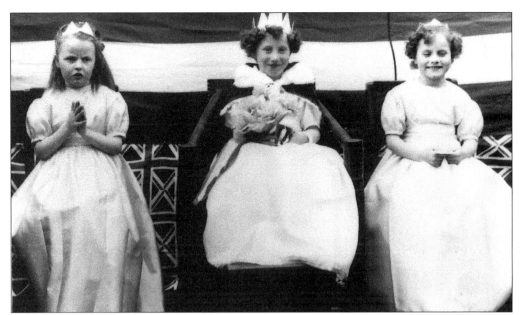

Woodhouse Street held a fancy dress competition to mark the Coronation of Queen Elizabeth in 1953. In this photograph, from left to right, are: Mary Corcoran, Judy Leigh and Margaret Horsley.

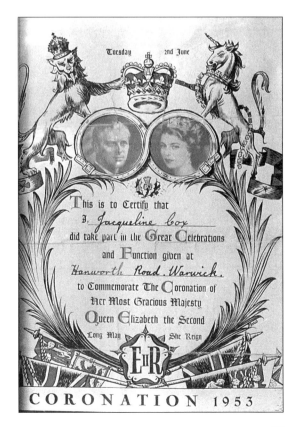

Hanwith Road also organised some celebrations for the 1953 Coronation and this certificate confirms that Jacqueline Cox took part in them!

Flooding at Oxstall Farm caravan park in 1950. The little boy is Jonathan Simpson.

John Cashmore enjoys a drink at the Tavistock Inn, in the 1950s. Behind the bar is Mrs Knight the landlady.

Mr and Mrs Pankhurst and a friend load their coats and bags into the family Ford outside their home in Hanworth Road before setting off for a holiday in Weston Super Mare in the 1950s.

Johnny Haynes and friend Albert won first and second prizes at the John Harris Tramps Ball on 27 January 1957.

A fashion show at Beauchamp School, in 1959. From left to right: June Haynes, Stall and Webby.

Warwick once boasted an open-air swimming pool among its attractions. Here is Betty Pyatt going for a swim in it in 1959.

The Eagle Flower Show in 1963. Mr R.J. Stanton (steward) discusses some of the finer points of flower judging with Mr A.W. Harwood, the judge (right). Mr Harwood, formerly of Priory Nurseries, was a fellow of the Royal Horticultural Society and a national dahlia judge.

The Priory Nursery stand at the annual Warwick Horticultural and Allotment Society show at St Nicholas Park in 1953.

Mr A.W. Payne admires the exhibits at the Imperial Foundry's first annual flower show at which he won the most awards.

June Hayes enjoys a day out with the Ford Popular in 1961.

This group of girls from Newburgh School sang and played together as the Palas Kats and were photographed at Birmingham airport in 1979. They are, from left to right: Tracy Boil, Anita Place, Sarah Harris, Sarah Hunt, Alison Barrow, Sian Matthews, Penny Hammond, Andrea Harris, Lara Davies, Kate Morgan.

Outside the entrance to Warwick racecourse. These gates and the building on the left are no more but the racecourse has always been a popular place for family walks. Betty Walters and Mary Groves and family went walking there on this day in 1960. The children are Philip, Richard (in the pushchair) and Susan.

The Warwick Corps of Drums led here by Father Christmas. Pat Walters was co-founder of the group which was photographed here in Church Street. The war memorial can be seen on the right, just past the Warwick library, which has since been relocated to Barrack Street.

Four

Growing Up in Warwick

This chapter contains a sequence of children's photographs taken in Warwick over the last hundred years. The children appear in all kinds of dress and settings and are arranged here, as far as possible, in date order. It is fascinating to see how differently, over the years, children have been presented for a photograph, according to the conventions of the time and the requirements of photographers, their parents and, in later photographs, of themselves.

A group of Warwick schoolgirls in fresh white pinafores and hats, 1890s.

Madge Lucas poses for her first portrait photograph in the early 1900s.

Mrs Oughton poses for a photograph with her new grandchild in the garden of her home in Parkes Street. This street has now disappeared and is the site of Sainsbury's supermarket.

Ten-year-old Maynard Greville, second son of the fifth Earl of Warwick, was photographed driving around the grounds of his home, Warwick castle, in this custom made, tiller-steered toy car in 1908.

A studio portrait taken in 1908 of the children of Mr and Mrs William Payne. From left to right they are: Alec, Elsie, Walter Florrie.

A class at Westgate school in Bowling Green Street, *c.* 1900. The school was opened in 1884.

Mrs Garrison and her children, Phyllis, Bill, Cyril and Sidney in 1915. This may have been a family picture taken for Mr Garrison to take with him to the front. Certainly the photograph was taken with the war in mind because the back of the photograph, which was produced as a postcard, is illustrated with pictures of all the flags of the Allies.

Ruth Fisher posed for this photograph while her father, John, held the horse.

Constance Bourton, her mother Maud and sister Helen photographed outside their cottage at Leadham in the late 1920s.

The Bourton sisters with their nanny Ruth Betts at Leadham in Henley Roadin around 1930.

Another nostalgic picture of rural life at Leadham in the early 1930s. Here at Leadham Farm the farmer's wife bends down to talk to her young visitors, the Bourton sisters, with Ruth Betts (standing on the left). The children are, left to right: Helen, Lillie and Constance.

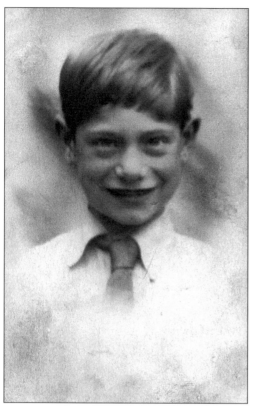

Alwyn Loveridge (above left) and sister
Gwendoline (above) photographed in a
Warwick studio in the 1920s.

Helen Bourton and a friend pose with their
pets in the early 1930s.

Muriel James seen here in 1928 when she played the part of Dandino in the Christmas concert at All Saints school.

Above left: Choir boys, Derek (left) and Don Austin, photographed in Lillington church, c. 1930. Don is a very longstanding member of the Leamington Operatic Society.
Above: Brother and sister, Roy and Joan Davies in 1938.

Elizabeth and Loraine Haynes playing in the garden at Newburgh Crescent in the late 1940s.

Warwick Girls Life Brigade at a holiday camp at Kessingland in the 1940s. Mrs Lawrence was the captain at the time.

Margaret Garrison in her Girls Life Brigade uniform in around 1947. She was also at the camp shown above.

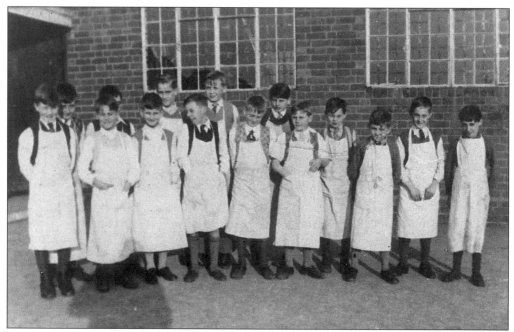

Milverton school woodwork class photographed in the late 1930s. The boys are, front row, left to right: Joe Vaughan, Ron Cashmore, David Wild, Geof Goulding, Frank Brown, ? Hopkins, Bill Reading, Frank Rawlings, 'Dickie' Wood. Back row: Denis Forth, Ray Wiggins (hidden), Cliff Holsey, Bob Cashmore, Gordon Clench, -?-.

Little Margaret Horsley, aged twelve months, is pictured with her big sister Betty in 1948.

Christine Garrison at three years of age on the garden wall outside the family home in Landor Raod in 1948.

The VE Day party in Hanworth Road, 1945. In this group are: Margaret Garrison, Wendy Palmer, Gina Baker, Gerald and Wendy Kennard, Terry and Pam Stretton, John, Barbara and Brian Hartsorne, Freddie Mabbet, Cherry Jones, Steven Morley, Joan Hughes, Kath Rigby, Evelyn Loveridge, Norma Hill, Joyce and Eileen Sponge, Rosemary and Barry Potter, Bet and Ron Cordwell, Delphine Hunt, Susie and Jimbo Round, June Hall, Sheila Pipkin, Kath and Tom Dolton, Rosetta Smith, Dot Jordan, Derek and John Hudson, Trevor Hardcastle, Pam Garrison, Pam Green, Barbara Rose, John Hammond, Mike Manley, Mike Hughes, Brian Tallett, John Wood, Jessie and Nina Woodhouse, Derek and Brian Howells and John Hardman.

School friends Ann Gardener (left) and Christine Garrison were photographed in the back garden in around 1948.

June Haynes is pictured here on her tricycle in the back garden in 1949. Tricycles like this were a common sight at the time, in fact, I had one myself!

A children's Christmas party in the early 1950s. Three children in the centre of the group are Frank, Margaret and Pam Gibbons.

Marilyn Haynes of Newburgh Crescent at twelve months of age. The pram complete with its fringed suntop is a typical design of the 1940s and 50s. These prams folded down to make a pushchair as well.

These three little bridesmaids attended Pat Jenkins when she married Derek Hopkins in 1952. They are, from left to right: Josie Jenkins, June Haynes and Marilyn Haynes.

The Cape celebrated the coronation of Queen Elizabeth in 1953 with a fancy dress competition in Hanworth Road. Linda Tallett and Gillian Cox dressed up as sailors in a boat. After the fancy dress the planned picnic tea outdoors was held in someone's garage because it rained!

Girls from Westgate school: Jean, Ruth and a friend, in 1956.

School friends: Richard
Walters, David (Danny)
Rawlins, Edward Chapman and
? Gwyn in 1967.

Westgate school juniors in 1972. I have fond memories of this school as not only did my sister, brother and I attend the school, but so did our mother before us! Among those in this photograph are: Stella Walters, Anita Pace, Mandy Hickman, Tracy Carter-Harris, Lisa Gwyn, Mandy Webb and Rebecca Coles.

Five
Warwick People

This chapter follows a similar idea to the last one but this time invites the reader to meet a selection of people who have lived and worked in Warwick, over the last century or so. They are not famous people, though you may well recognise some of them, but they have all made a contribution to the life of the town. Like the last chapter the photographs have been arranged in chronological order so that changes in style of dress, hairstyles and settings can be followed. The changing fashions of the periods when seen like this are quite distinct and often seem quite remarkable.

This wedding group was taken, probably in the garden of the bride's family, after Violet Cashmore married Cyril Carvell in around 1912. Cyril's brother Victor, who was a keeper in the park, was the best man. The lady sitting second from the right is Mrs Fanny Smith, the wife of Mr Smith of Cherry Orchard brickyard, Kenilworth and the tall man at the back is Herbert Merrick who worked on the railways.

The Cashmore family portrait, *c.* 1910. They are, back row, from left to right: Violet (bride of the previous photograph), Magdaline, George, Ethel, Marion. Front row: Florence, Samuel, John, Sarah, Frances.

The dapper Mr Frederick Bourton, a gardener. He holds a scroll of rolled paper in his hand for the portrait; has he just obtained his indentures as a qualified gardener? This, or some other significant achievement, may have been the reason for having this photograph taken.

Above and above right: Grandad and Granny Hemmings photographed outside their cottage over a century ago. They had six children; Emily, Anne, Lucy, Tom, Dick and Jack.

Great Granny Townsend in Paradise Street in the early 1900s.

Evelyn Percy and Charles Reeves were married at Hatton church in 1906. Evelyn was a charge nurse and Charles a senior charge nurse at Central Hospital.

Granny Edith Garrison lived at 2, North Rock and had eight children.

Gwen Gardener and William Loveridge on their wedding day in 1922. William was born in Warwick in 1897 and his bride was born in Satisford, Warwick in 1905.

The wedding of James Marshall Davies and Mary Elizabeth Fisher in 1928.

Gertrude (Trudie) Cashmore of Tavistock Street on a Sunday outing to the Lido on the river Avon, *c.* 1932.

The wedding of Marjorie Bagnall and Arthur Simpson in 1938. On the left is the best man, Clive Harrison and on the right are Arthur Bagnall and matron of honour, Evelyn Bishop. One of the little bridesmaids is Gwendoline Bagnall.

A studio portrait of Ivy Gibbons, aged twenty-five, in 1925.

Marjorie Bagnall in the bridemaid's dress she wore for the wedding of Madge Lucas in 1933. Marjorie was eighteen when this photograph was taken, five years before her own wedding which was seen on the previous page.

Sidney Garrison proudly shows off his four months old daughter Margaret in 1939.

These newly weds were photographed after their wedding in September 1939. The bride is Evelyn Reeves and the groom Stephen Kibbler, a senior charge nurse at Hatton Hospital. The war separated them soon after their wedding and they did not meet again until 1944. Traditional white weddings became a rare sight during the war years, and for some time afterwards too, because of shortages and the rationing of clothing materials. The photograph was taken at Malcolm McNeille's studio in High Street, Warwick.

The family group at Nellie Baker's wedding in the late 1940s. Nellie died tragically with her two sons in 1966 when her cottage in Radford Senele caught fire.

The wedding of Mr and Mrs Easterlow at St Pauls church in the late 1940s. Among the onlookers are Betty Pyatt, Margaret Horsley, Percy Copson, Margaret Brind, Hettie Hopkins, Mrs Arrowsmith and Bill Claridge.

Constance Bourton sat for this portrait in the 1940s. She worked as an accountant with Warwick County Council until her retirement.

A Walters family photograph taken in the back garden in Brooke Street in 1953. From left to right: Dad, Alex and Pat Walters. The children are John and Sheila.

Mr and Mrs Payne at their home in 1970. Mr Payne was a farmer and gamekeeper and lived well into his nineties. He was a well known fiddle player and played for concerts and dances in the area.